Data Science from Scratch

Comprehensive guide with essential principles of Data Science

Table of Contents

This document is geared towards providing exact and reliable information in regards to the topic and issue covered. The publication is sold with the idea that the publisher is not required to render accounting, officially permitted, or otherwise, qualified services. If advice is necessary, legal or professional, a practiced individual in the profession should be ordered.

- From a Declaration of Principles which was accepted and approved equally by a Committee of the American Bar Association and a Committee of Publishers and Associations.

The information provided herein is stated to be truthful and consistent, in that any liability, in terms of inattention or otherwise, by any usage or abuse of any policies, processes, or directions contained within is the solitary and utter responsibility of the recipient reader. Under no circumstances will any legal responsibility or blame be held against the publisher for any reparation, damages, or monetary loss due to the information herein, either directly or indirectly.

Respective authors own all copyrights not held by the publisher.

The information herein is offered for informational purposes solely, and is universal as so. The presentation of the information is without contract or any type of guarantee assurance.

The trademarks that are used are without any consent, and the publication of the trademark is without permission or backing by the trademark owner. All trademarks and brands within this book are for clarifying purposes only and are the owned by the owners themselves, not affiliated with this document.

INTRODUCTION

Data is a commodity, but without ways to process it, its value is questionable. Data science is a multidisciplinary field whose goal is to extract value from data in all its forms. This ebook explores the field of data science through data and its structure as well as the high-level process that you can use to transform data into value.

Data science is a process. That's not to say it's mechanical and void of creativity. But, when you dig into the stages of processing data, from munging data sources and data cleansing to machine learning and eventually visualization, you see that unique steps are involved in transforming raw data into insight.

The steps that you use can also vary. In exploratory data analysis, you might have a cleansed data set that's ready to import into R, and you visualize your result but don't deploy the model in a production environment. In another environment, you might be dealing with real-world data and require a process of data merging and cleansing in addition to data scaling and preparation before you can train your machine learning model.

Data comes in many forms, but at a high level, it falls into three categories: structured, semi-structured, and unstructured. Structured data is highly organized data that exists within a repository such as a database (or a comma-separated values [CSV] file). The data is easily accessible, and the format of the data makes it appropriate for queries and computation (by using languages such as Structured Query Language (SQL) or Apache Hive). Unstructured data lacks any content structure at all (for example, an audio stream or natural language text). In the middle is semi-structure data, which can include metadata or data that can be more easily processed than unstructured data by using semantic tagging. This data is not fully structured because the lowest-level contents might still represent data that requires some processing to be useful.

PREFACE

It's in all of us. Data science is what makes us humans what we are today. No, not the computer-driven data science this book will introduce you to, but the ability of our brains to see connections, draw conclusions from facts, and learn from our past experiences.

More so than any other species on the planet, we depend on our brains for survival; we went all-in on these features to earn our place in nature. That strategy has worked out for us so far, and we're unlikely to change it in the near future.

But our brains can only take us so far when it comes to raw computing. Our biology can't keep up with the amounts of data we can capture now and with the extent of our curiosity. So we turn to machines to do part of the work for us: to recognize patterns, create connections, and supply us with answers to our numerous questions.

The quest for knowledge is in our genes. Relying on computers to do part of the job for us is not—but it is our destiny.

CHAPTER ONE

DATA SCIENCE - DATA VS INFORMATION VS KNOWLEDGE

There could be three things possible when we consider a technical scenario: data, information and knowledge.

Some real facts that are stored in some physical medium may be termed as data. So maybe the traffic signal information and bus GPS data is getting logged somewhere into the database. If you run a simple query on that database, you would get list of columns with unique identifiers, numbers, timestamps and some ids. This could barely make some sense to the viewer. The bus crosses a signal is a fact and the log getting created is data. So what's the point in logging those alpha-numeric characters in a database, which grows at a rapid rate?

This is a very valid question, which is going to be answered soon. The database administrator has the complete idea of the database schema, column mappings, id mappings and other technical stuff.

He designs a complex query, which helps render a dataset that seems more nominal to be read, because he has simplified the data in a readable format. The report now has some columns like date, bus number, stop name, journeys and arrival time. This is something that makes more sense than rows of data that seemed Greek and Latin at the start. This is a transformed version of captured data that provides you the correct facts. This is the information that helps you understand the running of buses and at what time the next bus would come at the mentioned stop. Just a second, is it just for the information to the passenger that we are running a cluster of servers with a team of technical brains monitoring it? Every Monday morning, the project director of the bus services of the city, receives an automated mail that gives him a report of the complete bus system and how it performed the last week. It includes complete information right from the bus frequencies, stops occupancies, bus accidents, traffic information and much more. Now when he comes to know that there are 3 buses running on a route that has only 2 passengers coming every 3 hours, he can make the decisions to change the route of some buses, so that the stops overloaded with passengers could benefit from the empty running buses. This decision could be taken because he knew about the complete bus service system performance. Now that's smart isn't it? That is because he had the knowledge about the things through the reports he checked in his Monday mails.

Now there may be some non-tech people or may be some technical ones but not working with data, which may pop up with a question of extracting knowledge from data. It's easy to understand the logging of data and querying the database to get information. But imagine a bus system with 200 buses running across the cities, with each bus sending a signal every 5 seconds and each stop sending signals of arrival of each bus and also of its departure. Wouldn't that cumulate to crores of records in a week? Moreover, how would one read all those records and come up with a condensed report?

There's when something called business intelligence comes to place, which has got some intersection with data science. A lot of people say that business intelligence and data science are two completely different things, but factually, apart from reporting of historical data, the other segments of BI collaborate closely with data science to render useful analytics. So what is the word BI? It has been the buzz of the IT market for quite a while. If I go by the definition provided by the world's top consultancy giant (Gartner Inc.), "Business intelligence (BI) is an umbrella term that includes the applications, infrastructure and tools, and best practices that enable access to and analysis of information to improve and optimize decisions and performance." The defi nition seems to be tough for novices to digest, so I would surely take you through. Getting a deeper into the bus service system would help us understand the mentioned jargons easily.

Say for example, the bus service system has numerous bus operators, which design the bus schedules, routes and the journeys of the same. Generally, they define this in an excel spreadsheet which is easier to maintain and review. They give this to the bus services technical team by uploading the fi les to the FTP servers. This is the initial crunch of data that the team receives, for the first day of the week. Moreover, the buses generate signals every 5 seconds, to keep the system updated of their presence on the streets, which also helps them in monitoring the vehicles. A signal of every 5 seconds are amounts to some 3, 45,000 signals per day by the buses. There might be some 200 stops in the city, that report the system, the entry and exit of each bus on the stop in each journey, which may amount to some 3,00,000 signals per day. Considering the complete system with other logging mechanisms of tickets and passenger counts, the database could expect some 12, 00,000 records per day, which account to almost a crore per week. Remember the data given by bus service operators in the excel files? How would you include that as a part of your analytics? Also there might be data in flat files given by bus stops about their daily data in fl at fi les or CSVs. Even if the DBA (Database Administrator) dealt with such huge amount of data, how would he deal with data which is coming from different sources like CSVs, Excels, and Satellite data of the buses? Business Intelligence comes to rescue with its impressive ETL technology. The ETL or data Extract, Transform and Load, helps integrate the data from various data sources (which are not generally structured) into a single place. This helps us get data at one place to help us start perform analysis on the data. But still we have a problem. Billions of records are getting logged every week into a database. How could you store all of them into a single database? This would lead to a situation that can be termed as data explosion, where it becomes difficult to handle data. Moreover the query would take years to execute if you ran a complex query over some years of historical data.

Data Warehousing, a component of Business Intelligence helps us get this done. The load of the live database is reduced by archiving historical data in a data warehouse and letting the live data come into the production database. The data-warehouse is a copy of the transactional database that is restructured for analysis purposes (again using ETL). Still the data-warehouse is an OLTP database, which is not suitable for analysis. So, heard of OLAP cubes? The second and most important component of BI comes to the focus with the Analytical cubes. OLAP (Online Analytical Processing) cubes are BI components that store data in a compressed and pre-aggregated form that are helpful for running analytical queries. These cubes are structured in a way to store data in an optimized way. The cubes have capacity to store historical data of several years. Water in the well never helped to quench thirst of the thirsty. What we were concerned with was the knowledge to gain insights to make decisions. So the third front of BI off ers reporting services, which help represent the data through interactive reports. These reports help us get a bird eye view of the happenings of the business. This is the point where BI may bid good bye and let core data science take the center stage.

Going by the Wikipedia definition, "Data Science is the extraction of knowledge from data."

We now are well versed with knowledge and data. But the various techniques to get knowledge out of the stored information or data make this a subject of interest. Professionals working in the field of data science are termed as data scientists.

Applying data science techniques on data varies from case to case, and it needs to have a well-planned approach. There can be a general plan for performing data science over some datasets. Moreover, the data professional must be certain with the type of output that he wants after performing the required analytics.

The field of data science can be very interesting as it borrows a lot of things from a myriad of disciplines. There are techniques, algorithms and patterns derived from areas like Information theory, Information technology, mathematics, statistics, programming, probability models, data engineering, data modeling, pattern learning, predictive modeling and analytics, business intelligence, data compression and high performance computing. The predictive modeling, theories and models of data mining have added a lot to data science, as they have enhanced the predictive capabilities of the field.

THE DATA EXPLOSION

With the rise of technology and data storage systems, we have been able to log data into servers. Over the period of years, the cost of storage hardware has gone down, which has allowed IT companies to buy numerous commodity servers and storage systems to store data and also to extend data storage as a service to its clients. Content generated from analog systems inform of sensors, mobile devices, instruments, web logs and transactions has been digitized and stored. It's worth highlighting the fact that 90% of the data in the world today has been generated in the past two years. Data scientists have applied numerous techniques on this massive data to identify patterns that has added to the commercial and social value of humans.

This avalanche of data has led to inception of new technologies like that of Big Data, which help us perform our experiments better and quicker on the incoming data. Several high performance computing systems like that of Hadoop and Cluster computing have helped data scientists explore petabytes of data in a much quicker way than ever before. It is an additive for a data scientist if he is well-versed with big data technologies. Since a single person cannot be a jack of all trades especially in such complex projects, generally the data analytics team has several big data developers, administrators and architects on board to assist the core data scientists to expedite the analytics process.

FACETS OF DATA

In data science and big data you'll come across many different types of data, and each of them tends to require different tools and techniques. The main categories of data are these:

- Structured

- Unstructured

- Natural language

- Machine-generated

- Graph-based

- Audio, video, and images

- Streaming

Let's explore all these interesting data types.

STRUCTURED DATA

Structured data is data that depends on a data model and resides in a fixed field within a record. As such, it's often easy to store structured data in tables within databases or Excel files. SQL, or Structured Query Language, is the preferred way to manage and query data that resides in databases. You may also come across structured data that might give you a hard time storing it in a traditional relational database. Hierarchical data such as a family tree is one such example.

The world isn't made up of structured data, though; it's imposed upon it by humans and machines. More often, data comes unstructured.

UNSTRUCTURED DATA

Unstructured data is data that isn't easy to fit into a data model because the content is context-specific or varying. One example of unstructured data is your regular email. Although email contains structured elements such as the sender, title, and body text, it's a challenge to find the number of people who have written an email complaint about a specific employee because so many ways exist to refer to a person, for example. The thousands of different languages and dialects out there further complicate this. A human-written email is also a perfect example of natural language data.

NATURAL LANGUAGE

Natural language is a special type of unstructured data; it's challenging to process because it requires knowledge of specific data science techniques and linguistics.

The natural language processing community has had success in entity recognition, topic recognition, summarization, text completion, and sentiment analysis, but models trained in one domain don't generalize well to other domains. Even state-of-the-art techniques aren't able to decipher the meaning of every piece of text. This shouldn't be a surprise though: humans struggle with natural language as well. It's ambiguous by nature. The concept of meaning itself is questionable here. Have two people listen to the same conversation. Will they get the same meaning? The meaning of the same words can vary when coming from someone upset or joyous.

MACHINE-GENERATED DATA

Machine-generated data is information that's automatically created by a computer, process, application, or other machine without human intervention. Machine-generated data is becoming a major data resource and will continue to do so. Wikibon has forecast that the market value of the industrial Internet will be approximately $540 billion in 2020. IDC (International Data Corporation) has estimated there will be 26 times more connected things than people in 2020. This network is commonly referred to as the internet of things.

The analysis of machine data relies on highly scalable tools, due to its high volume and speed. Examples of machine data are web server logs, call detail records, network event logs, and telemetry.

The machine data would fit nicely in a classic table-structured database. This isn't the best approach for highly interconnected or "networked" data, where the relationships between entities have a valuable role to play.

GRAPH-BASED OR NETWORK DATA

"Graph data" can be a confusing term because any data can be shown in a graph.

"Graph" in this case points to mathematical graph theory. In graph theory, a graph is a mathematical structure to model pair-wise relationships between objects. Graph or network data is, in short, data that focuses on the relationship or adjacency of objects.

The graph structures use nodes, edges, and properties to represent and store graphical data. Graph-based data is a natural way to represent social networks, and its structure allows you to calculate specific metrics such as the influence of a person and the shortest path between two people.

Examples of graph-based data can be found on many social media websites For instance, on LinkedIn you can see who you know at which company.

Your follower list on Twitter is another example of graph-based data. The power and sophistication comes from multiple, overlapping graphs of the same nodes. For example, imagine the connecting edges here to show "friends" on Facebook. Imagine another graph with the same people which connects business colleagues via LinkedIn.

Imagine a third graph based on movie interests on Netflix. Overlapping the three different-looking graphs makes more interesting questions possible. Graph databases are used to store graph-based data and are queried with specialized query languages such as SPARQL.

Graph data poses its challenges, but for a computer interpreting additive and image data, it can be even more difficult.

AUDIO, IMAGE, AND VIDEO

Audio, image, and video are data types that pose specific challenges to a data scientist. Tasks that are trivial for humans, such as recognizing objects in pictures, turn out to be challenging for computers. MLBAM (Major League Baseball Advanced Media) announced in 2014 that they'll increase video capture to approximately 7 TB per game for the purpose of live, in-game analytics. High-speed cameras at stadiums will capture ball and athlete movements to calculate in real time, for example, the path taken by a defender relative to two baselines.

A company called DeepMind succeeded at creating an algorithm that's capable of learning how to play video games. This algorithm takes the video screen as input and learns to interpret everything via a complex process of deep learning. It's a remarkable feat that prompted Google to buy the company for their own Artificial Intelligence (AI) development plans. The learning algorithm takes in data as it's produced by the computer game; it's streaming data.

STREAMING DATA

While streaming data can take almost any of the previous forms, it has an extra property. The data flows into the system when an event happens instead of being loaded into a data store in a batch. Although this isn't really a different type of data, we treat it here as such because you need to adapt your process to deal with this type of information.

Examples are the "What's trending" on Twitter, live sporting or music events, and the stock market.

CHAPTER TWO

THE DATA SCIENCE PROCESS

SETTING THE RESEARCH GOAL

Data science is mostly applied in the context of an organization. When the business asks you to perform a data science project, you'll first prepare a project charter. This charter contains information such as what you're going to research, how the company benefits from that, what data and resources you need, a timetable, and deliverables.

RETRIEVING DATA

The second step is to collect data. You've stated in the project charter which data you need and where you can find it. In this step you ensure that you can use the data in your program, which means checking the existence of, quality, and access to the data.

Data can also be delivered by third-party companies and takes many forms ranging from Excel spreadsheets to different types of databases.

DATA PREPARATION

Data collection is an error-prone process; in this phase you enhance the quality of the data and prepare it for use in subsequent steps. This phase consists of three subphases: data cleansing removes false values from a data source and inconsistencies across data sources, data integration enriches data sources by combining information from multiple data sources, and data transformation ensures that the data is in a suitable format for use in your models.

DATA EXPLORATION

Data exploration is concerned with building a deeper understanding of your data. You try to understand how variables interact with each other, the distribution of the data, and whether there are outliers. To achieve this you mainly use descriptive statistics, visual techniques, and simple modeling. This step often goes by the abbreviation EDA, for Exploratory Data Analysis.

DATA MODELING OR MODEL BUILDING

In this phase you use models, domain knowledge, and insights about the data you found in the previous steps to answer the research question. You select a technique from the fields of statistics, machine learning, operations research, and so on. Building a model is an iterative process that involves selecting the variables for the model, executing the model, and model diagnostics.

CHAPTER THREE

COURSE ON PYTHON

Is there such a thing? Yes, there are a few Python courses for people who don't have programming backgrounds, but there aren't many, and their quality varies widely. Most Python training books and courses are aimed at people who already possess extensive programming skills, and are looking to expand the list of computer languages they're competent in. This is understandable, as the people most likely to buy a book on computer programming are experienced programmers, so that's who publishers and course organizers aim the bulk of their products at.

But what if you're someone who doesn't have a single bit of programming experience? Well, there are a few books and courses targeted for absolute newbies at Python, but their quality, and more importantly, their cost, varies widely. Online you'll find sites making claims that you can learn

Python in under fifteen minutes. That's absurd, of course; these sites are simply using headlines like those to get you to their page. Those claims aren't meant to be taken seriously.

At the other end of the spectrum there are boot camp style courses which take place over several days which promise to teach Python to beginners. Some of these are quite good, but there are a couple of drawbacks. For most people, it will cost several hundred dollars for transportation, food and lodging to attend the boot camp. Plus, these type of training programs usually cost a thousand dollars or more. For most people, this sort of expense simply isn't feasible.

Fortunately, there is a happy medium, and you don't need to shell out a thousand dollars to learn Python. There is one book which is written for people who don't know the first thing about programming. It uses bite size lessons, and in a little under 90 days will have you writing real programs in Python, and will give you a solid foundation for more advanced Python training.

Basic of python

What is Python?

Python is a powerful modern computer programming language. It bears some similarities to Fortran, one of the earliest programming languages, but it is much more powerful than Fortran.

Python allows you to use variables without declaring them (i.e., it determines types implicitly), and it relies on indentation as a control structure. You are not forced to define classes in Python (unlike Java) but you are free to do so when convenient.

Python was developed by Guido van Rossum, and it is free software. Free as in "free beer," in that you can obtain Python without spending any money. But Python is also free in other important ways, for example you are free to copy it as many times as you like, and free to study the source code, and make changes to it. There is a worldwide movement behind the idea of free software, initiated in 1983 by Richard Stallman.[1]

Python is a good choice for mathematical calculations, since we can write code quickly, test it easily, and its syntax is similar to the way mathematical ideas are expressed in the mathematical literature. By learning Python you will also be learning a major tool used by many web developers.

Installation and documentation

If you use Mac OS X or Linux, then Python should already be installed on your computer by default. If not, you can download the latest version by visiting the Python home page, at http://www.python.org where you will also find loads of documentation and other useful information. Windows users can also download Python at this website. Don't forget this website; it is your first point of reference for all things Python.

Running Python as a calculator

The easiest way to get started is to run Python as an interpreter, which behaves similar to the way one would use a calculator. In the interpreter, you type a command, and Python produces the answer. Then you type another command, which again produes an answer, and so on.

In OS X or Linux, to start the Python interpreter is as simple as typing the command python on the command line in a terminal shell. In Windows, assuming that Python has already been installed, you need to find Python in the appropriate menu. Windows users may choose to run Python in a command shell (i.e., a DOS window) where it will behave very similarly to Linux or OS X.

For all three operating systems (Linux, OS X, Windows) there is also an integrated development environment for Python named IDLE. If interested, you may download and install this on your computer.

For help on getting started with IDLE see http://hkn.eecs.berkeley.edu/~dyoo/python/idle_int Once Python starts running in interpreter mode, using IDLE or a command shell, it produces a prompt, which waits for your input. For example, this is what I get when I start Python in a command shell on my Linux box:

doty@brauer :~% python

Python 2.5.2 (r252 :60911 , Apr 21 2008 , 11:12:42)

[GCC 4.2.3 (Ubuntu 4.2.3 -2 ubuntu7)] on linux2

Type " help " , " copyright" , " credits" or " license" for more information.

>>>

where the three symbols >>> indicates the prompt awaiting my input.

So experiment, using the Python interpreter as a calculator. Be assured that you cannot harm anything, so play with Python as much as you like. For example:

>>> 2*1024 2048

>>> 3+4+9 16

>>> 2**100

1267650600228229401496703205376 L

In the above, we first asked for the product of 2 and 1024, then we asked for the sum of 3, 4, and 9 and finally we asked for the value of 2100. Note that multiplication in Python is represented by *, addition by +, and exponents by **; you will need to remember this syntax. The L appended to the last answer is there to indicate that this is a long integer; more on this later. It is also worth noting that Python does arbitrary precision integer arithmetic, by default:

>>> 2**1000

1 0 7 1 5 0 8 607 186267 320948 425049 060001 810561 404811 705533 6074437 50

3 8 8 3 7 0 3 510 511249 361224 931983 788156 958581 275946 729175 5314682
51

8 7 1 4 5 2 8 569 231404 359845 775746 985748 039345 677748 242309 8542107
46

0 5 0 6 2 3 7 114 187795 418215 304647 498358 194126 739876 755916 5543946
07

7 0 6 2 9 1 4 571 196477 6865421 676604 2983165 262438 6837205 668069 376L

Here is another example, where we print a table of perfect squares:

```
>>> for n in [1 ,2 ,3 ,4 ,5 ,6]:
... print n **2
...
1
4
9
16
25
```

36

This illustrates several points. First, the expression [1,2,3,4,5,6] is a list, and we print the values of n 2 for n varying over the list. If we prefer, we can print horizontally instead of vertically:

>>> for n in [1 ,2 ,3 ,4 ,5 ,6]:

... print n **2 ,

... 1 4 9 16 25 36 simply by adding a comma at the end of the print command, which tells Python not to move to a new line before the next print.

These last two examples are examples of a compound command, where the command is divided over two lines (or more). That is why you see ... on the second line instead of the usual >>>, which is the interpreter's way of telling us it awaits the rest of the command. On the third line we entered nothing, in order to tell the interpreter that the command was complete at the second line. Also notice the colon at the end of the first line, and the indentation in the second line. Both are required in compound Python commands.

CHAPTER FOUR

DEFINING FUNCTIONS

It is possible, and very useful, to define our own functions in Python. Generally speaking, if you need to do a calculation only once, then use the interpreter. But when you or others have need to perform a certain type of calculation many times, then define a function. For a simple example, the compound command

>>> def f (x):

... return x*x

... defines the squaring function $f(x) = x 2$, a popular example used in elementary math courses. In the definition, the first line is the function header where the name, f, of the function is specified. Subsequent lines give the body of the function, where the output value is calculated. Note that the final step is to return the answer; without it we would never see any results. Continuing the example, we can use the function to calculate the square of any given input:

```
>>> f (2)
```

4

```
>>> f (2.5)
```

6.25

The name of a function is purely arbitrary. We could have defined the same function as above, but with the name square instead of f; then to use it we use the new function name instead of the old:

```
>>> def square (x ):

... return x*x

...

>>> square (3)
```

9

```
>>> square (2.5)
```

6.25

Actually, a function name is not completely arbitrary, since we are not allowed to use a reserved word as a function name. Python's reserved words are: and, def, del, for, is, raise, assert, elif, from, lambda, return, break, else, global, not, try, class, except, if, or, while, continue, exec, import, pass, yield.

By the way, Python also allows us to define functions using a format similar to the Lambda

Calculus in mathematical logic. For instance, the above function could alternatively be defined in the following way:

>>> square = lambda x: x*x

Here lambda x: x*x is known as a lambda expression. Lambda expressions are useful when you need to define a function in just one line; they are also useful in situations where you need a function but don't want to name it.

Usually function definitions will be stored in a module (file) for later use. These are indistinguishable from Python's Library modules from the user's perspective.

FILES

Python allows us to store our code in files (also called modules). This is very useful for more serious programming, where we do not want to retype a long function definition from the very beginning just to change one mistake. In doing this, we are essentially defining our own modules, just like the modules defined already in the Python library. For example, to store our squaring function example in a file, we can use any text editor3 to type the code into a file, such as def square (x):

return x*x

Notice that we omit the prompt symbols >>>, ... when typing the code into a file, but the indentation is still important. Let's save this file under the name "SquaringFunction.py" and then open a terminal in order to run it:

doty@brauer :~% python

Python 2.5.2 (r252 :60911 , Apr 21 2008 , 11:12:42)

[GCC 4.2.3 (Ubuntu 4.2.3 -2 ubuntu7)] on linux2

Type " help " , " copyright" , " credits" or " license"

for more information.

>>> from SquaringFunction import square

>>> square (1.5)

2.25

Notice that I had to import the function from the file before I could use it. Importing a command from a file works exactly the same as for library modules. (In fact, some people refer to Python files as "modules" because of this analogy.) Also notice that the file's extension (.py) is omitted in the import command.

STRINGS

Other useful data types are strings (short for "character strings"); for example "Hello World!". Strings are sequences of characters enclosed in single or double quotes:

```
>>> " This is a string "
```

```
' This is a string '
```

```
>>> ' This is a string , too '
```

```
' This is a string , too '
```

```
>>> type ( " This is a string ")
```

```
< type ' str ' >
```

Strings are an example of a sequence type.

LISTS AND TUPLES

Other important sequence types used in Python include lists and tuples. A sequence type is formedby putting together some other types in a sequence. Here is how we form lists and tuples:

```
>>> [1 ,3 ,4 ,1 ,6]
```

[1 , 3 , 4 , 1 , 6]

>>> type ([1 ,3 ,4 ,1 ,6])

< type ' list '>

>>> (1 ,3 ,2)

(1 , 3 , 2)

>>> type ((1 ,3 ,2))

< type ' tuple '>

Notice that lists are enclosed in square brackets while tuples are enclosed in parentheses. Also note that lists and tuples do not need to be homogeneous; that is, the components can be of different types:

>>> [1 ,2 , " Hello " ,(1 ,2)]

[1 , 2 , ' Hello ' , (1 , 2)]

Here we created a list containing four components: two integers, a string, and a tuple. Note that components of lists may be other lists, and so on:

>>> [1 , 2 , [1 ,2] , [1 ,[1 ,2]] , 5]

[1 , 2 , [1 , 2] , [1 , [1 , 2]] , 5]

By nesting lists within lists in this way, we can build up complicated stuctures.

Sequence types such as lists, tuples, and strings are always ordered, as opposed to a set in mathematics, which is always unordered. Also, repetition is allowed in a sequence, but not in a set.

THE RANGE FUNCTION

The range function is often used to create lists of integers. It has three forms. In the simplest form, range(n) produces a list of all numbers 0, 1, 2, . . ., n − 1 starting with 0 and ending withn − 1. For instance,

>>> range (17)

[0 , 1 , 2 , 3 , 4 , 5 , 6 , 7 , 8 , 9 , 10 , 11 , 12 , 13 , 14 , 15 , 16]

You can also specify an optional starting point and an increment, which may be negative. For instance, we have

>> range (1 ,10)

[1 , 2 , 3 , 4 , 5 , 6 , 7 , 8 , 9]

>>> range (-6 ,0)

[-6 , -5 , -4 , -3 , -2 , -1]

>>> range (1 ,10 ,2)

[1 , 3 , 5 , 7 , 9]

>>> range (10 ,0 , -2)

[10 , 8 , 6 , 4 , 2]

Note the use of a negative increment in the last example.

Comments

In a Python command, anything after a # symbol is a comment. For example:

print " Hello world " # this is silly

Comments are not part of the command, but rather intended as documentation for anyone reading the code.

Multiline comments are also possible, and are enclosed by triple double-quote symbols:

""" This is an example of a long comment that goes on and on

and on ."" "

Numbers and other data types

Python recognizes several different types of data. For instance, 23 and −75 are integers, while 5.0 and −23.09 are floats or floating point numbers. The type float is (roughly) the same as a real number in mathematics. The number 12345678901 is a long integer ; Python prints it with an "L" appended to the end.

Usually the type of a piece of data is determined implicitly.

The type function

To see the type of some data, use Python's builtin type function:

>>> type (-75)

< type ' int ' >

>>> type (5.0)

< type ' float '>

>>> type (12345678901)

< type ' long '>

Another useful data type is complex, used for complex numbers. For example:

>>> 2j

2j

>>> 2j -1

(-1+2 j)

>>> complex (2 ,3)

(2+3 j)

>>> type (-1+2 j)

< type ' complex '>

Notice that Python uses j for the complex unit (such that j 2 = −1) just as physicists do, instead of the letter i preferred by mathematicians.

EXPRESSIONS

Python expressions are not commands, but rather form part of a command. An expression is anything which produces a value. Examples of expressions are: 2+2, 2**100, f((x-1)/(x+1)).

Note that in order for Python to make sense of the last one, the variable x must have a value assigned and f should be a previously defined function.

Expressions are formed from variables, constants, function evaluations, and operators. Parentheses are used to indicate order of operations and grouping, as usual.

OPERATORS

The common binary operators for arithmetic are + for addition, - for subtraction, * for multiplication, and / for division. As already mentioned, Python uses ** for exponentiation. Integer division is performed so that the result is always another integer (the integer quotient):

```
>>> 25/3

8

>>> 5/2

2
```

This is a wrinkle that you will always have to keep in mind when working with Python. To get a more accurate answer, use the float type:

```
>>> 25.0/3

8.3333333333333339

>>> 5/2.0

2.5
```

If just one of the operands is of type float, then the result will be of type float. Here is another example of this pitfall:

>>> 2**(1/2)

1

where we wanted to compute the square root of 2 as the 1

2

power of 2, but the division in the exponent produced a result of 0 because of integer division. A correct way to do this computation is:

>>> 2**0.5

1.4142135623730951

Another useful operator is %, which is read as "mod". This gives the remainder of an integer division, as in

>>> 5 % 2

1

>>> 25 % 3

1

which shows that 5 mod 2 = 1, and 25 mod 3 = 1. This operator is useful in number theory and cryptography.

Besides the arithmetic operators we need comparison operators: <, >, <=, >=, ==, !=, <>. In order these are read as: is less than, is greater than, is less than or equal to, is greater than or equal to, is equal to, is not equal to, is not equal to. The result of a comparison is always a boolen value

True or False.

>>> 2 < 3

True

>>> 3 <2

False

>>> 3 <= 2

False

Note that != and <> are synonomous; either one means not equal to. Also, the operator == means is equal to.

```
>>> 2 <> 3

True

>>> 2 != 3

True

>>> 0 != 0

False

>>> 0 == 0

True
```

CHAPTER FIVE

ANALYZING THE DATA SCIENCE

To practice data science, in the true meaning of the term, you need the analytical know-how of math and statistics, the coding skills necessary to work with data, and an area of subject matter expertise. Without this expertise, you might as well call yourself a mathematician or a statistician. Similarly, a software programmer without subject matter expertise and analytical know-how might better be considered a software engineer or developer, but not a data scientist.

Because the demand for data insights is increasing exponentially, every area is forced to adopt data science. As such, different flavors of data science have emerged. The following are just a few titles under which experts of every discipline are using data science: ad tech data scientist, director of banking digital analyst, clinical data scientist, geoengineer data scientist, geospatial analytics data scientist, political analyst, retail personalization data scientist, and clinical informatics analyst in pharmacometrics. Given that it often seems that no one without a scorecard can keep track of who's a data scientist, in the following sections I spell out the key components that are part of any data science role.

Collecting, querying, and consuming data

Data engineers have the job of capturing and collating large volumes of structured, unstructured, and semistructured big data — data that exceeds the processing capacity of conventional database systems because it's too big, it moves too fast, or it doesn't fit the structural requirements of traditional database architectures.

Again, data engineering tasks are separate from the work that's performed in data science, which focuses more on analysis, prediction, and visualization. Despite this distinction, whenever data scientists collect, query, and consume data during the analysis process, they perform work similar to that of the data engineer.

Although valuable insights can be generated from a single data source, often the combination of several relevant sources delivers the contextual information required to drive better data-informed decisions. A data scientist can work from several datasets that are stored in a single database, or even in several different data warehouses. At other times, source data is stored and processed on a cloud-based platform that's been built by software and data engineers.

No matter how the data is combined or where it's stored, if you're a data scientist, you almost always have to query data — write commands to extract relevant datasets

from data storage systems, in other words. Most of the time, you use Structured Query Language (SQL) to query data.

Whether you're using an application or doing custom analyses by using a programming language such as R or Python, you can choose from a number of universally accepted file formats:

» **Comma-separated values (CSV) files:** Almost every brand of desktop and web-based analysis application accepts this file type, as do commonly used scripting languages such as Python and R.

» **Scripts:** Most data scientists know how to use either the Python or R programming language to analyze and visualize data. These script files end with the extension .py or .ipynb (Python) or .r (R).

» **Application files:** Excel is useful for quick-and-easy, spot-check analyses on small- to medium-size datasets. These application files have the .xls or .xlsx extension. Geospatial analysis applications such as ArcGIS and QGIS save with their own proprietary file formats (the .mxd extension for ArcGIS and the .qgs extension for QGIS).

» **Web programming files**: If you're building custom, web-based data visualizations, you may be working in D3.js — or Data-Driven Documents, a JavaScript library for data visualization. When you work in D3.js, you use data to manipulate web-based documents using. Html, .svg, and .css files.

CHAPTER SIX

COMBINING DATA FROM DIFFERENT DATA SOURCES

Your data comes from several different places, and in this substep we focus on integrating these different sources. Data varies in size, type, and structure, ranging from databases and Excel files to text documents.

We focus on data in table structures in this chapter for the sake of brevity. It's easy to fill entire books on this topic alone, and we choose to focus on the data science process instead of presenting scenarios for every type of data. But keep in mind that other types of data sources exist, such as key-value stores, document stores, and so on.

The Different Ways Of Combining Data

You can perform two operations to combine information from different data sets. The first operation is joining: enriching an observation from one table with information from another table. The second operation is appending or stacking: adding the observations of one table to those of another table.

When you combine data, you have the option to create a new physical table or a virtual table by creating a view. The advantage of a view is that it doesn't consume more disk space. Let's elaborate a bit on these methods.

Joining Tables

Joining tables allows you to combine the information of one observation found in one table with the information that you find in another table. The focus is on enriching a single observation. Let's say that the first table contains information about the purchases of a customer and the other table contains information about the region where your customer lives. Joining the tables allows you to combine the information so that you can use it for your model.

To join tables, you use variables that represent the same object in both tables, such as a date, a country name, or a Social Security number. These common fields are known as keys. When these keys also uniquely define the records in the table they are called primary keys. One table may have buying behavior and the other table may have demographic information on a person.

Using Views To Simulate Data Joins And Appends

To avoid duplication of data, you virtually combine data with views. In the previous example we took the monthly data and combined it in a new physical table. The problem is that we duplicated the data and therefore needed more storage space. In the example we're working with, that may not cause problems, but imagine that every table consists of terabytes of data; then it becomes problematic to duplicate the data.

For this reason, the concept of a view was invented. A view behaves as if you're working on a table, but this table is nothing but a virtual layer that combines the tables for you.

Views do come with a drawback, however. While a table join is only performed once, the join that creates the view is recreated every time it's queried, using more processing power than a pre-calculated table would have.

Enriching Aggregated Measures

Data enrichment can also be done by adding calculated information to the table, such as the total number of sales or what percentage of total stock has been sold in a certain region.

Extra measures such as these can add perspective, we now have an aggregated data set, which in turn can be used to calculate the participation of each product within its category. This could be useful during data exploration but more so when creating data models. As always this depends on the exact case, but from our experience models with "relative measures" such as % sales (quantity of product sold/total quantity sold) tend to outperform models that use the raw numbers (quantity sold) as input.

CHAPTER SEVEN

MACHINE LEARNING

Do you know how computers learn to protect you from malicious persons? Computers filter out more than 60% of your emails and can learn to do an even better job at protecting you over time.

Can you explicitly teach a computer to recognize persons in a picture? It's possiblebut impractical to encode all the possible ways to recognize a person, but you'll soon see that the possibilities are nearly endless. To succeed, you'll need to add a new skill to your toolkit, machine learning, which is the topic of this chapter.

What is machine learning

The definition of machine learning coined by Arthur Samuel is often quoted and is genius in its broadness, but it leaves you with the question of how the computer learns. To achieve machine learning, experts develop general-purpose algorithms that can be used on large classes of learning problems. When you want to solve a specific task you only need to feed the algorithm more specific data. In a way, you're programming by example. In most cases a computer will use data as its source of information and compare its output to a desired output and then correct for it. The more data or "experience" the computer gets, the better it becomes at its designated job, like a human does.

When machine learning is seen as a process, the following definition is insightful:

For example, as a user writes more text messages on a phone, the phone learns more about the messages' common vocabulary and can predict (autocomplete) their words faster and more accurately.

In the broader field of science, machine learning is a subfield of artificial intelligence and is closely related to applied mathematics and statistics. All this might sound a bit abstract, but machine learning has many applications in everyday life.

Applications for machine learning in data science

Regression and classification are of primary importance to a data scientist. To achieve these goals, one of the main tools a data scientist uses is machine learning. The uses for regression and automatic classification are wide ranging, such as the following:

- Finding oil fields, gold mines, or archeological sites based on existing sites (classification and regression)

- Finding place names or persons in text (classification)

- Identifying people based on pictures or voice recordings (classification)

- Recognizing birds based on their whistle (classification)

- Identifying profitable customers (regression and classification)

- Proactively identifying car parts that are likely to fail (regression)

- Identifying tumors and diseases (classification)

- Predicting the amount of money a person will spend on product X (regression)

- Predicting the number of eruptions of a volcano in a period (regression)

- Predicting your company's yearly revenue (regression)

- Predicting which team will win the Champions League in soccer (classification)

Occasionally data scientists build a model (an abstraction of reality) that provides insight to the underlying processes of a phenomenon. When the goal of a model isn't prediction but interpretation, it's called root cause analysis. Here are a few examples:

- Understanding and optimizing a business process, such as determining which products add value to a product line

- Discovering what causes diabetes

- Determining the causes of traffic jams

This list of machine learning applications can only be seen as an appetizer because it's ubiquitous within data science. Regression and classification are two important techniques, but the repertoire and the applications don't end, with clustering as one other example of a valuable technique. Machine learning techniques can be used throughout the data science process, as we'll discuss in the next section.

Where machine learning is used in the data science process

Although machine learning is mainly linked to the data-modeling step of the data science process, it can be used at almost every step.

The data modeling phase can't start until you have qualitative raw data you can understand.

But prior to that, the data preparation phase can benefit from the use of machine learning. An example would be cleansing a list of text strings; machine learning can group similar strings together so it becomes easier to correct spelling errors.

Machine learning is also useful when exploring data. Algorithms can root out underlying patterns in the data where they'd be difficult to find with only charts.

Given that machine learning is useful throughout the data science process, it shouldn't come as a surprise that a considerable number of Python libraries were developed to make your life a bit easier.

Python tools used in machine learning

Python has an overwhelming number of packages that can be used in a machine learning setting. The Python machine learning ecosystem can be divided into three main types of packages.

The first type of package is mainly used in simple tasks and when data fits into memory. The second type is used to optimize your code when you've finished prototyping and run into speed or memory issues. The third type is specific to using Python with big data technologies.

Packages For Working With Data In Memory

When prototyping, the following packages can get you started by providing advanced functionalities with a few lines of code:

- SciPy is a library that integrates fundamental packages often used in scientific computing such as NumPy, matplotlib, Pandas, and SymPy.

- NumPy gives you access to powerful array functions and linear algebra functions.

- Matplotlib is a popular 2D plotting package with some 3D functionality.

- Pandas is a high-performance, but easy-to-use, data-wrangling package. It introduces dataframes to Python, a type of in-memory data table. It's a concept that should sound familiar to regular users of R.

- SymPy is a package used for symbolic mathematics and computer algebra.

- StatsModels is a package for statistical methods and algorithms.

- Scikit-learn is a library filled with machine learning algorithms.

- RPy2 allows you to call R functions from within Python. R is a popular open source statistics program.

- NLTK (Natural Language Toolkit) is a Python toolkit with a focus on text analytics.

These libraries are good to get started with, but once you make the decision to run a certain Python program at frequent intervals, performance comes into play.

Optimizing Operations

Once your application moves into production, the libraries listed here can help you deliver the speed you need. Sometimes this involves connecting to big data infrastructures such as Hadoop and Spark.

■ Numba and NumbaPro — These use just-in-time compilation to speed up applications written directly in Python and a few annotations. NumbaPro also allows you to use the power of your graphics processor unit (GPU).

■ PyCUDA — This allows you to write code that will be executed on the GPU instead of your CPU and is therefore ideal for calculation-heavy applications. It works best with problems that lend themselves to being parallelized and need little input compared to the number of required computing cycles. An example is studying the robustness of your predictions by calculating thousands of different outcomes based on a single start state.

- Cython, or C for Python—This brings the C programming language to Python. C is a lower-level language, so the code is closer to what the computer eventually uses (bytecode). The closer code is to bits and bytes, the faster it executes. A computer is also faster when it knows the type of a variable (called static typing). Python wasn't designed to do this, and Cython helps you to overcome this shortfall.

- Blaze—Blaze gives you data structures that can be bigger than your computer's main memory, enabling you to work with large data sets.

- Dispy and IPCluster—These packages allow you to write code that can be distributed over a cluster of computers.

- PP—Python is executed as a single process by default. With the help of PP you can parallelize computations on a single machine or over clusters.

- Pydoop and Hadoopy—These connect Python to Hadoop, a common big data framework.

- PySpark—This connects Python and Spark, an in-memory big data framework. Now that you've seen an overview of the available libraries, let's look at the modeling process itself.

CHAPTER EIGHT

WHEN DO WE NEED MACHINE LEARNING?

When do we need machine learning rather than directly program our computers to carry out the task at hand? Two aspects of a given problem may call for the use of programs that learn and improve on the basis of their "experience": the problem's complexity and the need for adaptivity.

Tasks That Are Too Complex to Program.

• **Tasks Performed by Animals/Humans:** There are numerous tasks that we human beings perform routinely, yet our introspection concerning how we do them is not sufficiently elaborate to extract a well defined program. Examples of such tasks include driving, speech recognition, and image understanding. In all of these tasks, state of the art machine learning programs, programs that "learn from their experience," achieve quite satisfactory results, once exposed to sufficiently many training examples.

• **Tasks beyond Human Capabilities:** Another wide family of tasks that benefit from machine learning techniques are related to the analysis of very large and complex data sets: astronomical data, turning medical archives into medical knowledge, weather prediction, analysis of genomic data, Web search engines, and electronic commerce.

With more and more available digitally recorded data, it becomes obvious that there are treasures of meaningful information buried in data archives that are way too large and too complex for humans to make sense of. Learning to detect meaningful patterns in large and complex data sets is a promising domain in which the combination of programs that learn with the almost unlimited memory capacity and ever increasing processing speed of computers opens up new horizons.

Adaptivity. One limiting feature of programmed tools is their rigidity – once the program has been written down and installed, it stays unchanged. However, many tasks change over time or from one user to another.

Machine learning tools – programs whose behavior adapts to their input data – offer a solution to such issues; they are, by nature, adaptive to changes in the environment they interact with. Typical successful applications of machine learning to such problems include programs that decode handwritten text, where a fixed program can adapt to variations between the handwriting of different users; spam detection programs, adapting automatically to changes in the nature of spam e-mails; and speech recognition programs.

Types of Learning

Learning is, of course, a very wide domain. Consequently, the field of machine learning has branched into several subfields dealing with different types of learning tasks. We give a rough taxonomy of learning paradigms, aiming to provide some perspective of where the content of this book sits within the wide field of machine learning.

We describe four parameters along which learning paradigms can be classified. Supervised versus Unsupervised Since learning involves an interaction between the learner and the environment, one can divide learning tasks according to the nature of that interaction. The first distinction to note is the difference between supervised and unsupervised learning. As an illustrative example, consider the task of learning to detect spam e-mail versus the task of anomaly detection. For the spam detection task, we consider a setting in which the learner receives training e-mails for which the label spam/not-spam is provided. On the basis of such training the learner should figure out a rule for labeling a newly arriving e-mail message.

In contrast, for the task of anomaly detection, all the learner gets as training is a large body of e-mail messages (with no labels) and the learner's task is to detect "unusual" messages.

More abstractly, viewing learning as a process of "using experience to gain expertise," supervised learning describes a scenario in which the "experience," a training example, contains significant information (say, the spam/not-spam labels) that is missing in the unseen "test examples" to which the learned expertise is to be applied. In this setting, the acquired expertise is aimed to predict that missing information for the test data. In such cases, we can think of the environment as a teacher that "supervises" the learner by providing the extra information (labels). In unsupervised learning, however, there is no distinction between training and test data. The learner processes input data with the goal of coming up with some summary, or compressed version of that data. Clustering a data set into subsets of similar objets is a typical example of such a task.

There is also an intermediate learning setting in which, while the training examples contain more information than the test examples, the learner is required to predict even more information for the test examples.

For example, one may try to learn a value function that describes for each setting of a chess board the degree by which White's position is better than the Black's. Yet, the only information available to the learner at training time is positions that occurred throughout actual chess games, labeled by who eventually won that game. Such learning frameworks are mainly investigated under the title of reinforcement learning.

Active versus Passive Learners Learning paradigms can vary by the role played by the learner. We distinguish between "active" and "passive" learners. An active learner interacts with the environment at training time, say, by posing queries or performing experiments, while a passive learner only observes the information provided by the environment (or the teacher) without influencing or directing it. Note that the learner of a spam filter is usually passive – waiting for users to mark the e-mails coming to them. In an active setting, one could imagine asking users to label specific e-mails chosen by the learner, or even composed by the learner, to enhance its understanding of what spam is.

Helpfulness of the Teacher When one thinks about human learning, of a baby at home or a student at school, the process often involves a helpful teacher, who is trying to feed the learner with the information most use-ful for achieving the learning goal. In contrast, when a scientist learns about nature, the environment, playing the role of the teacher, can be best thought of as passive – apples drop, stars shine, and the rain falls without regard to the needs of the learner. We model such learning scenarios by postulating that the training data (or the learner's experience) is generated by some random process. This is the basic building block in the branch of "statistical learning." Finally, learning also occurs when the learner's input is generated by an adversarial "teacher." This may be the case in the spam filtering example (if the spammer makes an effort to mislead the spam filtering designer) or in learning to detect fraud.

One also uses an adversarial teacher model as a worst-case scenario, when no milder setup can be safely assumed. If you can learn against an adversarial teacher, you are guaranteed to succeed interacting any odd teacher.

Online versus Batch Learning Protocol The last parameter we mention is the distinction between situations in which the learner has to respond online, throughout the learning process, and settings in which the learner has to engage the acquired expertise only after having a chance to process large amounts of data. For example, a stockbroker has to make daily decisions, based on the experience collected so far. He may become an expert over time, but might have made costly mistakes in the process. In contrast, in many data mining settings, the learner – the data miner – has large amounts of training data to play with before having to output conclusions

.

Relations to Other Fields

As an interdisciplinary field, machine learning shares common threads with the mathematical fields of statistics, information theory, game theory, and optimization. It is naturally a subfield of computer science, as our goal is to program machines so that they will learn. In a sense, machine learning can be viewed as a branch of AI (Artificial Intelligence), since, after all, the ability to turn experience into expertise or to detect meaningful patterns in complex sensory data is a cornerstone of human (and animal) intelligence. However, one should note that, in contrast with traditional AI, machine learning is not trying to build automated imitation of intelligent behavior, but rather to use the strengths and special abilities of computers to complement human intelligence, often performing tasks that fall way beyond human capabilities. For example, the ability to scan and process huge databases allows machine learning programs to detect patterns that are outside the scope of human perception.

The component of experience, or training, in machine learning often refers to data that is randomly generated. The task of the learner is to process such randomly generated examples toward drawing conclusions that hold for the environment from which these examples are picked. This description of machine learning highlights its close relationship with statistics. Indeed there is a lot in common between the two disciplines, in terms of both the goals and techniques used. There are, however, a few significant differences of emphasis; if a doctor comes up with the hypothesis that there is a correlation between smoking and heart disease, it is the statistician's role to view samples of patients and check the validity of that hypothesis (this is the common statistical task of hypothesis testing). In contrast, machine learning aims to use the data gathered from samples of patients to come up with a description of the causes of heart disease.

The hope is that automated techniques may be able to figure out meaningful patterns (or hypotheses) that may have been missed by the human observer. In contrast with traditional statistics, in machine learning in general, algorithmic considerations play a major role. Machine learning is about the execution of learning by computers; hence algorithmic issues are pivotal. We develop algorithms to perform the learning tasks and are concerned with their computational efficiency. Another difference is that while statistics is often interested in asymptotic behavior (like the convergence of sample-based statistical estimates as the sample sizes grow to infinity), the theory of machine learning focuses on finite sample bounds. Namely, given the size of available samples, machine learning theory aims to figure out the degree of accuracy that a learner can expect on the basis of such samples.

There are further differences between these two disciplines, of which we shall mention only one more here. While in statistics it is common to work under the assumption of certain presubscribed data models (such as assuming the normality of data-generating distributions, or the linearity of functional dependencies), in machine learning the emphasis is on working under a "distribution-free" setting, where the learner assumes as little as possible about the nature of the data distribution and allows the learning algorithm to figure out which models best approximate the data-generating process. A precise discussion of this issue requires some technical preliminaries.

CHAPTER NINE

DATA VISUALIZATION

The increase in data size, type of data, data stream or batch, and the data structure is one of the issues in big data processing. Computer processing has a different method and approach based on the data characteristics. It will become complicated for the data scientist to deliver the processing plan. There is also a need to understand the business process, information architecture, information system design, data structures, and delivery system designs. In the term data science, we need to define the business process that should be used to deliver the information. The data science needs the word of knowledge to define business process. The data that come from different sources is managed together in the store and arranged in structured or unstructured formats.

The information architecture specifies the detail of data and information. The structure is used to define the data feature in the first process and the results. The information system design needs to know the information structure to describe the process and related information. The interaction between information architecture and information system design requires establishing the process. The data architecture manages the data science collection by identifying the data details, in this case metadata and content. The data processing method can deliver in several ways, such as integration, offline by using tools, online by using web application, and hybrid by using them in combination. The processing technology approach uses real-time, batch, and stream. The method and technical approach are combined based on the purposes.

The research investigates cloud-based processing in data process for data science visualization. The research designs the cloud-based processing steps for managing the data. The technology approach used in this study are cloud-based applications such as Google Drive, Google App Engines, and Google Fusion. The study uses the financial-banking data in Indonesia provided by Open Data Indonesia. The research goal is to deliver the data science visualization of intercitynetwork bank in Indonesia. This research has a contribution to the methods of cloud-based processing for data visualization as a best practice to deliver the data knowledge on particular issues. The paper has the following sections: Section II presents the current approach and method for data visualization. Section III delivers the step-by-step method on cloud-based processing. Section IV shows the result and discussion. The last section shows the conclusion and future direction.

Ii. Data Science Process And Visualization

The primary issues in data processing and display are big data and data science research, such as machine learning, data mining, semantic web, social networks, and information fusion. The research is based on an investigation and discovers a new technique in data processing, data representation, pattern mining, data storage, and visualization.

The combination of the algorithm and the process approach is the primary concern to the resulting information. The big data and little (small) data management can combine to support many purposes. The use of little (small) data as a sample and generated to answer a question has been used for many reasons. The little (small) data can be used for defining the sample of the big data. It will improve the quality of data and the process itself. The big data will enable in spreading data and enhance the quality of the sample and results.

Data management for long-term use and access, especially for big data, is an important issue in managing the data value and usage. Data processing has the capability to address the problem of long-term access and use, not only in the present but also in the future. Data processing for big data can be done by using distributed data mechanism at the storage and and work management levels. The technique of distributed data storage can increase the efficiency when provided through an Internet-enabled environment. The mechanism supports the system architecture for cloud-based processing. Data science needs an enormous volume of resources. In several cases, the processing needs to share with other resources to enhance capacity. The shared resources become the big data services that need protection. An authentication scheme is implemented to protect user privacy on the research conducted by Jeong and Shin. Big data processing focuses on end-to-end processing of data science integration, model, and evidence. The approach delivers by process mining and bridges the gap between data science and process science. The process mining use big data technologies, service based and cloud services.

The big data system architecture consists of several components, that is, data visualization, processing (include real-time, structured database, interactive analytics, and batch processing), data structure, and infrastructure. The data visualization in big data science delivers the intelligence visualization. The intelligence visualization displays information and knowledge. The real-time process, analytics, and batch processing need to address speed, reliabilities, and data spread especially in processing purposes. The data is classified into structured and unstructured data. The infrastructure needs to address the high-performance infrastructure to support the processing needs.

Emergency management is used in the case study and helps in overcoming the trending issue in emergency management. The visualization has been used to describe the difference between the type of record and history based on the provenance. The research is an organizational framework to specify the origin and design knowledge on it. Reactive Vega has presented a system architecture for graphic visualization and interaction. The research constructs the data flow graph, scene graph, and interaction with streaming data. The display has been built with the help of time scale, relational, and hierarchical data.

Iii. Cloud -Based Processing

This section talks about the research design and works. The research was divided into several steps such as data preparation, storage management, data processing and manipulation, data integration, and data visualization.

A. Data Sources

The research uses the data from Indonesia Open Data portal. Open Data Portal (data.go.id) is a data portal built by the Indonesian Government to establish the open data movement and free data service. The open data portal itself has 1042 datasets, 31 institutions, and 18 groups of data. The research uses economic and financial data, provided by the Bank of Indonesia. There are 153 datasets consisting of economic and financial information from a broad range of regions in Indonesia.

B. Data Preparation

The data preparation uses the data bank locator, operation, transaction volume, and economic indicators. The data preparation has several steps; there is data normalization, data cleansing, and data tagging Data normalization standardizes the data. The normalization identifies the region name, the bank office, the name of the bank, and the region classification.

Data cleansing is done to minimize the data error in geotagging and relation. The data cleansing process consists of taking a data sample of at least 30 items of data. The data is transformed into the visualization prototype. The process is to figure out whether there are data items that cannot be processed based on the current data.

Data tagging has two options. Geotagging is used to give location information to the data object such as location, bank office, and transaction data. The second option or geolocation uses Google Map API facilities to attach to it.

C. Storage Management

The cloud-based processing is stored the data and the process in the Internet facilities. The research uses Google Drive to place the data, Google App Engine to access the data stored in the intermediate storage and database engine, and Google Fusion to process the data and visualize it.

D. Data Processing and Manipulation

The data processing and manipulation have several steps: card process, mapping, chart, and summary. The data proceed first into the card. In this process, the data are collected into the record. The data become an individual item that will be used to continue the relation and data network.

The data is also used in the mapping process. The data uses the location parameter by rendering and process to have geolocation based on Google Map. The mapping process resulted in a card that had the information location. It also processes the transaction data. The next process is a chart and summary. The process is used to create a relation between datasets to map the network process. The summarizing will give weight to every data and the bank location to visualize in the representation burden.

E. Visualization

The visualization process works to display all the information that resulted from previous steps appropriately.. The visualization process itself has a particular format. The process identified the bank institution and location (city) as primary nodes, and transaction and other data as weight and give the value of nodes. Table I shows the visualization process. The visualization process is rendered from the dataset and displayed in the HTML format.

Iv. Result

The research has resulted in a working visualization prototype for displaying the bank, location, and transaction weight based on the cloud-based processing. The display shows the network maps chart.

The visualization result demonstrates the bank, location, and the transaction. The nodes have a different size based on the transaction weight on it. The visualization can be dynamic and comes out with the other data. The visualization can display the network between the banks that operate in several cities.

Data Science: Bar Charts AND Line Charts

Graphs and charts condense large amounts of information into easy-to-understand formats that clearly and effectively communicate important points. In selecting how best to present your data, think about the purpose of your graph or chart and what you want to present, then decide which variables you want to include and whether they should be expressed as frequencies, percentages, or categories.

When yo decide what kind of graph or chart best illustrates your data, you should consider what type of data you are working with. Categorical data are grouped into non-overlapping categories (such as grade, race, and yes or no responses). Bar graphs, line graphs, and pie charts are useful for displaying categorical data. Continuous data are measured on a scale or continuum (such as weight or test scores). Histograms are useful for displaying continuous data.

Bar graphs, line graphs, and histograms have an x and y-axis. The x-axis is the horizontal part of the graph and the y-axis is the vertical part.

Types f Graphs and Charts

•   A bar graph is composed of discrete bars that represent different categories of data. The length or height of the bar is equal to the quantity within that category of data. Bar graphs are best used to compare values across categories.

•   A line graph displays the relationship between two types of information, such as number of school personnel trained by year. They are useful in illustrating trends over time.

•   A histogram has connected bars that display the frequency or proportion of cases that fall within defined intervals or columns. The bars on the histogram can be of varying width and typically display continuous data.

Guidelines for Formatting Graphs and Charts

•   Keep it simple and avoid flashy special effects. Present only essential information.

Avoid using gratuitous options in graphical software programs, such as three-dimensional

bars, that confuse the reader. If the graph or chart is too complex, it will not clearly communicate the important points.

•   Title your graph or chart clearly to convey the purpose. The title provides the reader with the overall message you are conveying.

•   Specify the units of measurement on the xand y-axis. Years, number of participants trained, and type of school personnel are examples of labels for units of measurement.

•   Label each part of the chart or graph. You may need a legend if there is too much information to label each part of the chart or graph. (See the line graph). Use different colors or variations in patterns to help the reader distinguish categories and understand your graph or chart.

CHAPTER TEN

MANIPULATING DATA

Data types

Computers can only deal with numbers and so the data we see and use has to be in the form of numbers when a computer system is using it. To make processing, e.g. calculations, sorting, etc., run faster and be less complicated for the processor to carry out, we assign store forms of data in different ways – we call these data types.

There are a number of different data types commonly used by computer systems, each type being used for a particular form of data:

Text: this is the most commonly used and text data can be any character such as letters, numbers, punctuation, space and other characters such as &, £, % and so on. Examples of text data are First Name, Family name, such as Brian Gillinder. If data is stored as text, we cannot carry calculations on the data. This data type can be known as alphanumeric.

Numeric: this data can only be numbers; either whole numbers or numbers with decimal places. Whole numbers are called integers while numbers with decimal places are often called real numbers. Numbers can be displayed or formatted in different ways, e.g. 234.89 is an example of a number with decimal places (a 'real' number) and can be displayed or formatted as £234.89 which is currency. Numbers with decimal places are also called floating point numbers and such numbers are more complicated for the computer to store and process than whole numbers, which is why there are the two data types for numbers.

Boolean or Logical: this data can have only two values, TRUE or FALSE.

Capturing data

Data capture is the process of collecting data for use in a computer system. Data can be captured in many ways but, however it is done, the data must be in a form that the computer can understand and use, otherwise it is useless. Data capture is collecting data ready to be typed into a computer, making measurements that can be typed in and asking people for information that can be entered into a computer system.

Data capture should not be confused with data entry. Data capture is the collection of data while data entry is the process of inputting the data into the computer. Although they may occur at almost the same time and may appear to be happening all in one go but they are quite separate processes, e.g. a barcode scanner will collect the data from a printed barcode (data capture) and send it to the computer terminal, e.g. at a supermarket checkout (data entry) to be processed. The result of the processing is shown on the checkout terminal or printed on the customer receipt.

The method of capturing data depends on what the data is going to be used for and where it is being collected. Sounds can be captured with the use of a microphone, or input directly from, e.g. a music keyboard using a midi interface, and new still and video images can be captured with digital cameras. Scanners can be used to capture or input documents or printed images such as photographs and graphic tablets can be used to draw new images on a computer.

Some data is captured automatically without much involvement by humans once the system is set up and working.

• Barcodes and magnetic stripes hold data that is captured by a reader or scanner.

• Optical character recognition reads data from documents and converts it into text on a computer ready for use.

• Optical mark readers gather data from pre-printed forms which have been marked up.

• Radio frequency identification (RFID) is used to track or identify objects which have had a chip implanted, e.g. a pet or a product and, increasingly, baggage carried on aircraft.

- Voice recognition is used to turn speech into computer data so that a voice or speaker can be identified or the spoken words entered into a word-processor for editing.

- Sensors can gather data for use by computers.

When we want to use data that we have collected ourselves, we should collect the data in a way that makes it easy for us to enter it into our computer system so data capture needs careful thought before it starts.

A common method of capturing data is to use a data capture form. This can be a simple tally sheet that is used to count, e.g. the number of vehicles passing a road junction or a long, complex questionnaire that collects data on people's background and educational history when applying for a job.

A commonly used data capture form is a questionnaire and these are useful when we wish to collect a lot of data from many people and do not have the time to talk to everyone in person. Also, questionnaires allow people to fill them in privately and in their own time.

A good data capture form should be designed so that it:

- is simple and easy to use, i.e.:

- only asks for the data that needs to be captured and not ask for any unnecessary information

- has a minimum of printed text or instructions

- is not too long

- is not boring to read!

- provides clear instructions on:

- what to do and how to fill in the form

- where to send or hand in the form

- has the spaces to be filled in as close to the questions as possible

- is logically laid out so that questions follow on from each other

- collects the data in a way that be quickly and easily entered into the computer system

- has the reason for the data capture clearly shown so people know what the data is to be used for.

The same sort of care should be taken over the design of all the forms, printouts and screens that are used by computer systems.

Any form that appears on screen should:

• be logically laid out so that the reader moves from one item to another in the normal reading manner, i.e. from left to right

• be suitable for use, or be adjustable so that it can be used, on different size monitors – not everyone has a large, high-resolution display!

• not be cluttered with too many items of information

• only have items that are relevant to the topic

• have text that is in a suitable typeface and font, e.g. size

• have text and images placed in suitable positions so as not to distract from the topic in question

• have clear instructions on how to use the screen or have access to a help screen

• not use colours that are difficult to see or tell apart – persons with colour vision problems may not be able to read red text on a green background, or bright yellow on red background may be dreadful to look at by some people

• have a simple and consistent method of moving between screens.

Similarly, forms and documents printed on paper should be carefully designed so that the reader finds them easy to view and use. With paper documents, room should be made for any headers or footers, and for the possibility that the pages may be stapled together, e.g. leave a gap on the side of the page so when several are stapled together the text is not hidden.

When printing booklets or books, gaps must left on alternate left and right edges so that the pages can be bound together without hiding the words.

When making a flip-over calendar, the gaps have to be at the top and bottom of alternate pages – so we need to think about the final product before we start.

Designing files for storing data

Most users of ICT systems never have to worry about how, or even where, their data is stored because the software application or the operating system will do it for them. If you are designed a database, then you will need to consider the layout of the fields and the number of tables and how they are linked but rarely do we bother with considering how the file is stored on, e.g. a hard disk. But this is important even though most are unaware that the designers of the software will have taken great care to ensure that data is stored securely and safely and can be easily retrieved.

Example

In a library, to find a book with a title beginning with P using serial access you would start at the first book with a tile starting with A and look at all the titles until you came to those starting with P and continue until you found the one you wanted. It could take a long time. With random access you would go straight to the book you wanted. Random access is also called direct access.

Designers of software that stores data need to consider:

- the type of storage medium to use, e.g. a hard disk or a removable optical medium or flash memory; a database needs fast rewriting or data would run very slowly using a small USB flash memory stick so most designers assume that the user has a hard disk for their data

- how the data is to be accessed, e.g. is it by random access or by serial access?

- how the data is to be grouped, e.g. related data should be grouped together and data that is not to be used often can be stored away from that in constant use; a TV set-top box for digital TV recordings has to have software that constantly monitors this so that any video files are properly stored to ensure smooth playback of movies, DVDs for movies have to have their files carefully arranged for the same reason

- how the data is linked together so that users can search for or extract data quickly and easily

- the number of accesses to files should be kept to a minimum by careful arrangement of the data files on disk so that the hard disk is not constantly searching for data all over the disk

• it should be possible to add or delete data. Checking data It is important that any data that is used is the data that we want to be used.

When capturing data it is our responsibility to make sure that we put the right questions on the data capture form so that we get the sort of answers that we can use.

We should always make sure that the data we collect is accurate and correct – computers cannot do that for us. If we collect data on the data capture form that is wrong, e.g. if we ask a person's age and write down 45 years instead of 54 years or we record a temperature of 21 degrees Celsius instead of 12 degrees Celsius there is no way that the computer will know that the data is wrong. This is one reason why measurements are made by sensors instead of recording them manually but some data cannot be recorded by sensors.

Once the data has been collected and we have checked that it is correct, e.g. we have the age of the person correctly recorded, the data can be entered. Often it is typed in by the user at a keyboard. This can introduce errors and mistakes as typing is slow and laborious and needs a great deal of concentration.

The first check that should be made on any data that is being entered is to make sure that the data being entered is the data that we want to be entered, e.g. we are typing what to appear in our document, spreadsheet or database. There are many ways that errors can occur when entering data from a data capture sheet including:

- the data may not be read properly from the data capture sheet

- a typing error may occur, e.g.:

- a spelling mistake

- data may be omitted, e.g. 2 instead of 12

- the same data may be entered twice, e.g. 11 instead of 12

- characters may be switched around, e.g. 21 for 12 or 'fats' instead of 'fast'

- an extra character may be added, e.g. 20 instead of 2

- typing the wrong character, e.g. when typing fast T might be entered instead of Y because the wrong character on the keyboard was hit

- rarely, there may be a faulty input device sending the wrong data to the computer.

This means that a check on the data typed into the document compared to the data on the data capture sheet has to be made. This is verification.

Verification

Verification is the process of making sure that the data that appears in a document or database is the same as the original source data on the data capture sheet.

When entering a small amount of data, it is sufficient to check the data by reading the source document and comparing it with the data in the computer system – this is a visual check. Visual checks only pick up transcription errors and do not detect inaccuracies in the original data.

When there is a large amount of data to be entered from many source documents, such as those used in, e.g. creating payrolls for paying wages, visual checks cannot made as the data has to be entered very quickly and there isn't time. In this case, it is much faster to have two data entry clerks typing in the same data and the computer will compare the two sets of entries. Any differences in the entries are reported to the clerks for correction. This is known as double entry.

Visual checking should not be confused with proof reading even though it would seem to be similar.

Proof reading

Proof reading is the reading through of documents to check for factual and other errors. Proof reading should be done by someone other than the original author and is used to spot inaccuracies in the facts and layout as well as any spelling or grammatical errors that may have gone unnoticed.

A proof reader will mark up a document and send it back to the author for corrections to be made. Proof reading does not check the data against the original source data that was collected.

When proof reading an electronic document on a computer, these symbols cannot be used. Find out what facilities a word processor will provide for a proof reader to mark up a document.

Validation

Validation is the process of checking that the data being entered, usually into a database or spreadsheet, is acceptable and reasonable. Validation is carried out by the computer according to rules set by the designer of the database who decides on what sort of data is wanted in the database or spreadsheet.

Again, validation does not check that the data is correct or accurate but checks that it is sensible and meets any rules that have been set up. For instance, if the age of a person is to be entered, then the database can check that the age is sensible by setting rules such as 'the age must be over 0 years' so a minus value cannot be entered, or the age must be over 18 years so that an age of 18 or under 18 years will be rejected.

Validation can be a powerful way of ensuring that only reasonable or sensible data is entered into a database.

There are a number of useful validation checks that can be set up and these include the following.

Range check

This checks that a value is in a given range. Range checks can be simple, e.g. a number is between 18 and 65, or a date is between, e.g. 4th April and 1st September, or can be quite complicated checking, for instance, that the date entered in February is not over 28 or 29 depending whether or not it is a leap year.

Format check

This is sometimes called a picture check and makes sure that the individual characters in the data are valid, e.g. no numbers in a name, no letters in numerical data or that there is the proper mixture of the two in, e.g. a vehicle identity number (VIN).

Since 1981, VINs have always had 17 characters not containing I, O or Q (so that these are not confused by readers with numbers) arranged in a format that records details of the manufacturer, model and serial number of the vehicle in a complicated sequence of letters and numbers. A format check will ensure that only valid letters and numbers are entered in the correct positions in the sequence.

In the UK, a National Insurance number must be in the format XX 99 99 99 X and the first two and the last characters must always be letters. All the other six characters are numbers with the total length always nine characters. If any other format is entered the computer system will reject it with an error message.

Length check

This checks that the correct number of characters have been input, e.g. a date must always have six characters such as 01/01/01 or must have eight characters such as 01/01/2001. It can also can determine maximum length of the data, e.g. those of phone numbers.

Presence check

Sometimes a rule can be set to ensure that a piece of data is always entered. This is a presence check but as it is not really checking the data but checking to see if it is there, some people do not regard this as a true validation check.

However, it is useful to make sure that all the required data is entered and is often seen on web pages where specific details, e.g. a contact telephone number, must be entered and must not be left blank.

Check digit

Some data is very complicated, such as the VIN mentioned above, so it has to be checked extremely carefully. Check digits are extra digits added to the end of codes such as product codes, bar codes, bank account numbers which must be entered correctly every time. The value of check digits is determined by the values and positions of other digits and characters in the code and are calculated when the data is entered and compared to a stored value. If the checks match then the data is accepted, if not an error is generated.

Validation checks must be created before any data is entered into a database or spreadsheet. Often, a field in a database can be set only to accept data of a certain type, e.g. only numbers can be entered, and this is often used as a simple validation check. It is not a flexible method of validating data but can be useful.

Thank you for reading this book!

www.ingramcontent.com/pod-product-compliance
Lightning Source LLC
Chambersburg PA
CBHW070844070326
40690CB00009B/1686